OF EDUCATION

10/6

AGAINST THE CRUEL FROST

For my Father
and his new family

Home is where one starts from. As we grow older
The world becomes stranger, the pattern more complicated
Of dead and living.

T. S. Eliot, *East Coker*

By the same author:

Children's Games
Imaginings
English for Maturity
Llareggub Revisited
Lights in the Sky Country

AGAINST THE CRUEL FROST

A Second Volume of Verse by

David Holbrook

PUTNAM
42 GREAT RUSSELL STREET
1963

CONTENTS

SEASONS

LOVE

TIME AND PLACE

ACKNOWLEDGMENTS

A Moth in a Morning has been published in *The New Statesman*; *She in the High Street* in *Delta*; *To His Wife in Bed* and *Cardoness Castle* in *Unicorn*. The poet is grateful to the Editors for permitting the publication of these poems here. He is grateful to Douglas Brown for help in making this selection.

SEASONS

MARCH BLIZZARD

So many kinds of snow, in this last unease
Before two weeks of March shall bring us to unthink it!
Here's a thick blizzard now: but yet the willow tree's
Yellow and warm, and crowds of starlings drink it,

Hail-pillule stuff: but then it changes, dark
Fat flakes fly upwards. Yet the jackdaws flock
Carrying home beak-booty, and all calling 'Jack!'
Into the thicket by the Mill. Snow-stuck,

The landscape's grey and white again awhile,
But then the sky clears, and the children walk
Marks on the stuff that squeaks under the heel,
Roll up emaciated snowmen by the brook.

Soon the paths melt, and the massed snowdrops' heat
Unclothes their doomed late petals, green and grey
Among the snow's brief brilliance where they meet,
Winter and spring, on this uncomfortable day.

But the old grey reign's broken, and a sudden coup
Due to come with the cuckoo—only six weeks to go:
Try all he can, no death grip binds the hope
Where the snow bites at blossom up against the blue.

Even the thickest fall, dark stipple in the sky,
Is braved by mobs of birds that babble, build,
Talking out Winter, feeling like you and me
Promise emerging best where the contest's most wild!

DREAMS OF RUIN

I had two vivid dreams. One, lighting a stove,
I dropped my comb behind fire-bars—symbol of my self-love,
It turned to clouds of mist, which, rising in the flue
Thundered and flashed. Running outside with you
Carrying our children, we saw our household fall,
The timbers burning in the rubble of our every wall.

And then in some strange house, talking to a girl,
My haunter who returns, vividly in the cool
Evenings alone in quiet places, or on a path, there,
Suddenly I see her feet approach, a light spray in her hair;
The woman, I suppose, one quests for all one's life
And seldom finds, even in the sweetest satisfaction of a wife.
She asked for someone whom we knew, old woman, dead
After an intimate *causerie* by her fireside that we had,
Showing me her family album girlishly, as if she knew
The Messenger would touch her door that night, and so
Could afford a little sentiment for once. So 'Where's
Phyllis?' asked the girl. 'She's dead', I said, 'for years'.
She and the landscape stiffened, meaningless and drear,
Her spirit faded, only the reckless equinoctial gale blew there,
And I was left alone. But tossed and flattened still
Growing, glowed green and flame wild crush-mouthed daffodil
Swaying upon their stems among our feet, and yet
The cruel wind unrelenting there would not remit.

ON AN OVERGROWN PATH

One summer's difference, between the clean
Spring spikes, the daffodils, and this
Choked October perplexity we begin
To tear from the bankside—withies
Tall as a child, willow, ash, sycamore;
The grass run everywhere we grope;

Nettle roots eaten into the barn floor
Between the bricks; the bindweed chains rope-
Wound over dry dead trunks; briars
Thick as a thumb and long as linen lines;
And woody nightshade berries' crimson fires
Hung in the dead espalier apple's ruins.
You and I stung ourselves and tore
This wild sun crop away from primroses,
Bared the black narcissus soil and swore
Next spring should pay in flowers for our bruises;
Wheeled away stacks of stuff to pipe in fires,
Or rot in a brown corner, chrysalis-filled,
Leaving the pool path looking much more like ours,
One summer's green sewn dragon's teeth well pulled.

But as we pause and kiss I look behind
And mark the path exposed, the damp sunk brick
I laid once, running over in my mind
What one had said, who never now will take
This path he loved again, who used to say
It looked as if it led to some enchanted lake.
Remembering this spring, too, when another lay
Dying, and here I fled the harrowing
Image of his unconscious hoar, in flowers.
I sadly break away and go back to my barrowing
To clear this nowhere-leading path of ours,
Many stings, spines and thorns away: and now
The dark tilth waits the frost, and here and there
I see a spike in place, buds formed, a few,
As their ideas survive them. Then a fair
Girl calls, grieving for her father still, and we
Offer what warmth we can, sharing the memory
Uncovered with the path that grows obscurity
Over itself, and pain and loss, as if deliberately.

SONG OF THE SEASONS

In summer when the lanes are green
And white with umbelliferae
The sickle rips the columbine
And nettles wither where they lie.

The autumn dahlias at the Mill
Drop scarlet as the conkers fall;
Frosty chrysanthemums still smell,
Late sunflowers wax against the wall:

In winter only garden shrubs
Furtively bloom with half a hope;
The Christmas roses hang bruised cups,
Bryony winds for heliotrope.

Spring's underfoot with aconite,
Then the elms smoulder with a rich
Rose haze; then snowdrops shiver, white;
Crocuses break beside the spawning ditch;

And soon the daffodils are mad
Again in April gales; in gallops May
With burst of apple, hail, and candle-gad;
Then summer languishes again all day.

(From *Superest Plebs Pessima*)

NIGHT SONG

Stack the cups and clear away;
The bonfire sinks to ash;
Daytime is so much trash,
Night climbs the stairway.

We have done what we can to use the light,
Cricket and jar take over;
Children snore, the smell of clover
Tickles the poacher's nose as he treads it over

Poppy and rose swim in the warm remainder,
Exhausted current of day;
Cold comes down from the air, hay
Hears warm in the field what the lovers say.

Bare to the teeming black the heady tree
Sighs in its sleep and stirs;
Softly an owl-wing whirrs,
The water chuckles, the paper beetle burrs.

Stack the cups and clear away,
The bonfire sinks to ash;
Daytime is so much trash,
Night climbs the stairway.

A MOTH IN A MORNING

The heat is breaking up, touches of yellow
Curl under the apple trees or catch the poplars,
Just catches, signs of turn, the mellow
Matching with flurries in the night, the rustlers
Tapping on lights or drumming on the panes.
'Too late! Too late!' thus cry huge dying female
Spiders that lurch across the walls. 'No gains!'
They cry, dropping from beams. Dozens of pale
Moths glare with their pink eyes, a flurry
Finishing summer, lightning flickering, the rains
Gathering in September mists. 'Come hurry!'
The first leaves fallen say. And yet today
I see in the waning humid light, so brave,
A single, papery, half-broken moth make way,
White in the morning, on wings summer gave,
In an uncertain moment, as the storms rise over there,
Describing an irregular life-hope, hovering, in her small air.

MOTHER NATURE, MOTHER TIME

(On Therfield Heath)

There is a sterner creature in the brakes
And life with you, sweetheart, has grown so bland
I'm insulated from her, sometimes, her exigencies and aches;
Yet she sweeps round, in the October wind,

And cries out in the glow under the stripping tree,
Her hand clutching the branches as they grey and thin,
And when I walk the heavy dew, in front of me—
Her foot has bruised the high turf deep within.

I must go back to her, and her embrace
Alone on the pond bank where, brief, clear, cold,
She holds the sky's light over the one free place
In all the matted water; or flings up that gold

Tall afterbreath of sunset that fades with the dark.
Do not be jealous if I must belong
To this great woman ghost whose pictures lurk
In the sky's country, long scene, or the song

Given this late lit day, on a chalk hill
By one small lark, over the tall dead bents
That like a sparse white bristle overall
Clothe the high downs. And my three innocents

Dive in this grass pelt as I run for them.
They disappear. I pause. And far away
The autumn slant light falls upon her hem
As she sweeps past, the bents bow to her way,

Cruel chill upon those children in the hill,
As though they'd never been, we'd never met,
I'd never middle-aged, nor yet grown fat,
No book-back faded. Yet the lark sang still

With the boy sound as when I used to lie
On warm wet turf like this, by such blue flowers,
Watching her stately presence in the sky,
Hearing her hoppers buzz, and smell her hay for hours.

Then thirty years passed as the breeze swept on,
The children leapt up, booed, and ran down hard;
She left us, and they, panting, fell again,
To watch pass by a thundering old Dad

Run like a boy, after his sometime Muse
Who now hurled in the beeches by the road and stirred
Bright mustard by a copse, leaf-lifting rose
To raise a migrant cloud that flew as one dark bird

Rather than thousands, as her bitter times
Return across that littered landscape. They run down.
We go to join you, their young mother, in the town,
And glowing from my chase I hear her toll the midday chimes.

WINTER SUNDAY

So severe this black frost that it bent
The white burred burden of asparagus,
Hooped the old docks and broke the thistle's spent
Grey screws of spike and floss.

They lay rimed in their torment in each bed;
And as an epilogue
I heard a voice speak, and I turned my head
Only to see a leaf fall in the fog

Down the drained sycamore, like a withered hand,
Bough by bough, to the earth. No sound
But these few vacant yellow cackles, and
A dripping where the frost's grip was unwound.

The day went by expressionless and dead,
Winter-oppressed, and in the afternoon
We tasted his dark will, as foul and sad
The smoke-thick cloak came prematurely down.

Our boundaries unseen, the tree still speaks,
Dry word by ominous word,
Blackly of our decay: then the news breaks
Of a man in the fog, crashed dead on the road

Not far from us. I go to fetch a child
Anxiously in the gloom: the streets are blank,
Only each chapel and the church are filled
With artificial light, where the hymns thank

Behind tall pointed windows, and the hot stove's steam.
The only other lamps are in the butcher's shed
Where he kills for next day. And where a scream
Shakes the thick mist, where, in a breeder's yard,

Men urge a monstrous boar to mount a sow,
Their cold breath plumes, their raucous shout
Drowning the hymns, and the half-stifled low
Where the doomed cattle in the shambles wait.

Then the black damp falls suddenly, reveals
This winter grip as but a trick of light
To make us introvert: now as the great Belt wheels
Daughter and I return, breathe happily of night.

But I still taste old winter's intercourse of airs
That makes us swallow in the thing we are
Who breed and kill and feed and say our prayers
Against the cruel frost, against the voices of the sycamore.

A DEATH IN WINTER

For the shade of Henry Morris

The cold today has squeezed the ice from paving
In thin clear tongues; even the grass is crisp,
Though the sun shines, as I walk grieving
For a while in the garden where he used to clasp

My arm, exclaiming on the beauty of the tower
Behind the weeping trees, and gesture at the path
Where the clear water streams by in the hoar.
My children cry as they go running round, their breath

Visible in the glowing December air.
It is my daughter's birthday; she is eight.
I'm hearing him exclaim upon her baby hair,
But he is ashes now, and calling Kate

Does not remember the old man who came
Occasionally here, till he was shut away:
Nor does her elder sister, only that his name
Makes her blush, because, we say, one day

She passed him on the stairs, naked, at four:
'They don't care, do they, at that age?', he said.
This is the house, at this kind of tea hour
He used to call: now he has joined the dead

Who have said at our table, 'When I am gone', or 'Yes,
I do fear death.' Now we are all at tea,
Every young apple face in a clean dress,
You are at work in candlelight, and busy me

Avoiding the old man's lonely ghost which, newly dead,
Wanders bent bowed in fog as the light wanes,
Eyeing our windows sadly as once alive he did
Asking after the extent of your last birth pains.

ASH

There will not now be much more joy than we have known,
Occasional felicities between our sheets, or teeth,
When by some chance no ghost foils our soar down.

Nor shall we ever be without some check upon our breath,
To know, say, that a child in sickness may not turn,
Nor shall we always come back to clear brow from death,

While bitter threads pervade the timbers of our gain
And the frost eats each wall that granulates, thawing:
The flounce of silk on flesh is rarer here than pain,

And sullen, unalloyed, what's won is won passing
As rough-cast patches fall, leaving the saffron pied,
Month by month, from the house, the years closing.

The walls, the stone, the clad, no purchase petrified,
But a defence withheld, in a long stuff process
That pits and crazes faces as it does each brick that's laid.

I reconcile myself, therefore, to seminal decay
Its spring signs in the garden in the barren time
Before the first Forsythia of February

14

And find no healing in no flaunted blossom flame
But in the unearthly-coloured ashes that I dig,
Orange and lilac paste where an old plum became

A pyre that sank to ash, covered with waste and rag:
And the tree stump I axe, intense amber disease
Intrinsic in the wood; and where the rot-pile's dug

Bright madder thongs of new blue nettle ties
Bleached to the tips, brown and flesh pink damp worms
Fat as boys' follies, red hairy roots of trees,

And in the wall, as if worked in with thumbs,
Whorls and bright fans of lichen, ochre, blue,
Brightening green and sulphur as the sunlight comes—

These are the dull time's flowers, these a bouquet for you
From me at Valentine when, digging thoughts of death,
I turn a rotted sack up where my probing spade must go,

Trenching for next month's tilth. And crouching down below
Where black rosettes of bonfire charcoal glow
Among the scattered ash, I find a solace in the mildew snow.

LOVE

SHE IN THE HIGH STREET

In the street's common long perspective
It shocks me that your body occupies
So little of the scene, a small objective
Distant, whose every gesture is familiar to my eyes.

For now, at the best times, this body, small and lithe,
Becomes my total world, all about me,
And from its pulse and flutter, stir and breathe
Is my world coloured: this dichotomy

How shall I reconcile, between your colour touch
Dot in a far shop door, and that all's swagged and chained
Gold sun-touched stuff, zenith to tree-top, rich,
Because my apprehension's with your sweetness stained?

EXHAUSTED STORM

Surely the tranquillest sight in all the world
These broken shreds of storm, hung indigo:
Orange to jewel blue the sky shows through
Rags and wind-eaten rain, lilac, and curtain-curled;
And now the rain beats down, and great
The rainbow's double hoop sweeps high up there,
Foreign and unfamiliar-hued, because so late.
And still the sun's fire struggles over here
While one west window's flame to muted mauve,
South's azure, washed; all darkening, and fast
Heavy rain tosses heads of shiny leaves
And green to black all agitates: and last
The poplars bow to the old passing storm
While blackbirds panic. Then the silence comes
To the damp stage-set garden with its flood-lit calm,
Thunderless dark falls, and July resumes
Her troubled summer passage.

But this vision, gone,
We did not share. This left it shreds and water,
Alien lights and steam: no more: no luminous paragon
Hung heaven-halls of you, summer's Miranda daughter:
No Ferdinand, I, on magic new-seen isles,
As it might have been. Common bad weather, refraction,
No rich and rare-for-lovers whiles,
But only sullen eyes in some unvisionary faction.
And like this storm, that wrecked and flashed in West lands,
Then soared to feathers of ice-cirrus curds,
Enfeebled vapour, lets the sky show through, unwinds
Its youthful spruce and danger—so do we evaporate,
today, in bitter words.

ROBES LOOSELY FLOWING, HAYRE AS FREE

'A sweet disorder in the dress,' wrote Herrick once
Of the 'tempestuous petticoat', and Jonson of the grace
In sweet neglect's simplicity. These I repeat
Of your young woman's scents you leave behind, and nothing
    neat—
Our rumpled bed, our towels and night-clothes, left
With a train of topless lotions where you, in your shift,
Did yourself up to catch the early train, cologne
Mixed with the smell of woman's flesh and smell of love. Alone
I only have the faint aroma of you, gone: and here
Ponder the sweetness of my all night in your hair,
And the confused disordered wantonness
Of this our married life. Then, taking up a dress
In the chill morning where the wardrobe creaks
And the cold chimneybreast sweats, now there breaks
Forth cruel comprehension from the hand that lifts
Your discard covers—how it will be when one
Stands in silent contemplation of all giving being done.
For these sweet rapturous indulgences that stir
Our living days, tempestuous, or quiet where
Our calm security lies tenderly in bed
Needing no breathless haste to undo or be sped—

C   17

These shall be gone to join the silent girls
Who become grey and hollow eyed, whose curls
Lie now with separated bones, fragments of linen thread
In a sweet-smelling dust—whom Jonson took to bed,
Or Herrick lay with gaily, shoe-string-tie bewitched:
And none can rise again, love, once that last free robe is stitched.

TO HIS WIFE IN BED

If this were all behind us, and regret
Lived but with memory, spurred by the set
Of another figure, or a shadow touching
Off old familiar home, my verse a reaching
Into a puzzled loneliness like Hardy's,
The long life's circumstance a goliardeys
Grimacing behind curtains—if we were parted,
Or you were dead—would they come so then, these dark-hearted
Pangs that come when we are most together?
Not at station barriers, in rain, or picnic weather,
But as tonight I hold you in my arms, in such close love
Before we put the light out. Strive
As I can, this is where sorrow falls: you arch
Your contented back and cry, 'What's wrong?'—such
Tangibility has the cloudfall. 'Nothing's wrong', I say—
Only that when I hold you thus I feel us slip away;
And while our bed's secure, our love affair
A daily rhythm following whether your hair
Is finely fingered up, or blows wind-wayward, or
Just falls across your face while polishing our floor,
We're parted daily, much as by travel-stops or grave.
Time subtly scars us unbeknown: he'll have
Us, somehow.
        And so, while other poets recall storms,
Girls calling out 'Beware', a terra-cotta dress, the forms
Of women riding by on beaches or by gates—I say, look here—
Our death's in every duster—here, my dear,
The frock I took you to the Boat Race in now scours the brass;
This yellow stuff recalls an orchard-sudden grass-

Marriage we made one spring—now shifts soft twill:
Even the garment that I met you in is somewhere still,
Lining a cushion. In our rag-bags, on our racks,
In the attic glory-hole, scatter evocative bric-à-bracs,
Small mundane monuments to us who wear away. The beast
That tears them never loves nor sleeps, as we must. So, a feast
Of eye alone's no end, neither for how much I love you, nor
For greedy sorrow: let me tomorrow say you wore
This short lawn nightshirt, and your eye was green,
As some round ferny spring, one New Year's Day, and then,

DROUGHT

So, we're estranged again—how it goes on!
Your who-you-are dissolved: my disappointed me
Skulking in silence. Rain falls, then it is gone.
The sun's bright on wet roofs, every washed tree
Has June's hard highlights, while a rivulet
Runs down the road that has been dry a month.
And with it run the feelings that I let
Flow as I contemplate our last dry month.

We have been very close, we have been sweet,
Fresh, active, despite flaws, and our old rout
Of masked ghost predators. Perhaps tonight
Some sudden shower again will break our drought?
Both of us are, I know, in our sorrow,
Watching the same rain from our each window.

CONTINUITY

The botanist must sigh and be prepared
To count the weeping willow's hanging trails
Leaf upon leaf. Or if we dug and bared
The pulp-grey wasps' nest with its many cells,
Each queen's fertility we could compute—
Would we come nearer a significance?
Each musty nutshell, every vocal brute,
Volitionless cells, vibrate in a death dance.

The autumn spells bewildering falls of all
Natural life has flung at keeping on—
Leaves heap, bare willow sleeps, frost makes a pall
For wasp corpse, apple: swallow, squirrel gone.
Against this dissolution, fecund, hide
Queen in my heart, for all the rest is dead.

HARVEST

Unwilling to wait until his fruit shall fall
The moorcock climbs the tree where the sunk pit
Of sweetness in the russet, wasp's awl
Carved, opens: with the greed of it
The slight tree shakes, the black wings reinstate
Balance for the bird, the branches give,
He scrambles, pecks: precarious and too late
This meal from summer's bounty to the thief.

Anxiously thus I mount your slightness dear,
Anticipate your flesh climacteric:
My wasp, unbalanced, flutter biting there
Anticipates and claws our threatened lack.
Teach me to let our awaited fruit to go
Parted from stem to mouth, willingly, so.

20

SPRING SONG

Inceptual bursts of song,
Bud points grown definite,
The willow yellow softening,
Bark shows the life in it.

A blustering warm stir
In the withy clusters:
Surprising the foot here
The snowdrop musters.

No need to idealise
To break our winter;
The sap cannot but rise,
Wild trumpets enter.

Generous blossom blow
Inevitable now,
And all that we can do
Is to live with this new

Gale that at Valentine
Stirs in your breast and thigh
Under this touch of mine,
Not impelled anxiously

But hesitant, for spring:
Petal is such thin stuff
It mars in handling.
Gentle rain is enough

For spring's bewilderment,
For this bud glimmer:
The ripening full torrent
Comes in the summer.

21

My daughter sat on my lap in green,
She wouldn't keep still, she swung her hair
So fine, long, dark with a bright child shine,
And laughed herself rose pink under there.

Her long lashes curling out, her eyes
Smoked naughtily, and flickering thought
Ran in her face as luminaries,
Her freckled cheeks like little trout.

I held her waist and loved the child
And felt her subtle skeleton,
And seven years' satisfactions thrilled
My solar plexus that she wriggled on.

'Do you love that man best, or me?'
'You are my father,' Katey said,
Holding her green arms like a tree,
Then winding them about my head.

This absolute reality I held
A moment tight and dark, and Kate was still,
Except for her quick heart that wild
Beat quickly, I could hear and feel.

Then green she flew in flounces off
Across the carpet where she once
Took her first step, here where our love
Caught Kate created in the long flesh dance.

Now as I clear the tea, in the March gloam
The children play like ghosts outside;
Kate baby is a ghost, Kate child, this nestling home
A passage only where child spirits ride.

22

I see another ghost, Kate as a bride;
I feel myself arrive with her in arms,
Only to turn to give her back her child
That she has brought to stay at its grand-mam's—

She writes or comes to stay: our scattered ones
Are seldom here again as this home-whole
That clatters in the kitchen all at once.
—This must be so, this must be so. Cruel!

Crueller to cling like bind to that green thing
That flies about the house until it knows
This is the time to take fulfilment's wing
And love and leave the love-hold where it grows!

So here I swallow, now they're all in bed,
My separation from what just now I held,
Warm in my lap, her arms about my head,
And learn to let her go, separated,

Mine but not mine! You and I, only two,
One day shall sit here, quietly, in Time,
And you shall ask me why I'm looking so—
As if I held a child's ghost, murmuring her name.

TIME AND PLACE

CARDONESS CASTLE

(adm. 6d; 10–4, Sun. from 2) a splendid 15th cent. tower
(View)

The keeper stopped the mower on the lawn,
Pocketed a stray dead leaf, sixpence, and
Our compliments on his neat gardens, graciously,
And led us to the ramp. Here in a siege
They brought the horses in; here were the stores;
And once the sea came to the very motte.
Romantic, noble pile; we gazed and saw
Appropriate horseman, rugged warriors,
Clan proud to war with clan, historic ghosts.

But these too literary unrealities stayed there outside
Beneath the painted signs about the monument.

Inside we took a tour of human evil: here
Above the door a grating: small greedy brutes
Lured in their confidences, and then split their skulls,
Or charred their guests' brains out with molten lead.
Step further: in the wall a privy, cut
So that one ostler sat above another, jeering, near
An oubliette, where, dropped fifteen feet down,
Languished the captured enemy, oppressed, evicted—those
With 'dangerous' ideas—and through the castle wall
A hole at which they dangled rich hot food
To taunt those dying, or extract by thirst
'Confessions', secrets, names—and then destroyed
The turncoat wretches. From the vertiginous tower
Numbers had been thrown: before the stone fireplace
Dark wiry bloodsoaked men had writhed in pain
Whom no despairing linen-tearing lady there could save,
While from the slits shot arrows into trunks, while
Maid-servants cowered in sweaty rush-floored rooms,

24

And rats slid hungrily from enemy to tower
Where spilt blood, oatmeal, gunpowder and wine
Ran to the seadrains from the suffering cruel
Dangerous brown men, howling their uncouth tongue.

We came out in the sunlight where the grass
Shaved short, a harmless green, hid decayed pits and graves
Where lay those creatures' bones. And could pretend
Life was now orderly and neat, with flowers:
No daggers at our throats, no human herds
Unprivate closeted in exhausted keep alcoves.

Till we took up our morning newspaper
In the car, with the maps, again, and saw
THREE IN A PRISON CELL: on the same page, VICTIMS'
    HANDS
TROPHIES IN TRIBESMEN'S BELTS, and everywhere
More perfect treachery without such weathered stones,
Protecting purlieus by poisoning the marrow in all bones.

OUT OF THIS WORLD. I

Jacob's Ladder

A wave broke, ran, and fell, and a net of sanded surf
Swept up the beach to die, leaving a fleck of scurf,
Bubbles, fine fern, damp green and coral wrack. Gone
The gather, roll, the break, the tumble, the glad run.

And yet the sea spoke on, and wave after bucking wave
Ran in like Leander to die between the shingle and the cave,
And time I walked the beach I overwalked my time
Spread out in overlacing waves under the red cliffs' climb.

Running in like a wave I am, not a white horse at sea
Bucking then pond again: this dark wind-shivered me
Rides on an undertow in middle age, and rising proud
Brinks over towards the shore, the tossed edge of the flood.

The slack lines of my verse
Stretch beyond gathering:
I can say nothing terse,
Cut no knot flower to endure weathering
In a stone pared circumference.
My art sits dumpling down
Swears that it will not dance:
I'll whip you, sir, on this cliff's crumbling crown,
We have not far to go—
Hop before this incentive.
Look down! Doesn't this vertigo
Bring out your plaintive
Appolyon wail, your trance
States, your touch with tragic
Truth? On this cracked edge dance,
Fortify your euphoric magic
By the gulls' thermal glide,
Or samphire's reckless bloom;
Tomorrow the landslide;
In winter the greedy boom;
Today the summer flower.
The cliff path's firm enough
For you to climb an hour
At the pitch of the bluff
All you need do is sing,
Here while we walk,
From nowhere to nothing,
An interlude of gay talk
Between the days when winks
Sun sweltering sea, or swept
Spray clouds the cliff-face, or
Brinks against sandstone, even this overleapt,
At times, by the sea's tongue: till then
Sing us a little sanity again.

The Ideal Holiday

We have been on the woods and the moors, resort to resort,
Dammed streams, dug springs, run surf, been boating,
And yet no solace comes. Once or twice I caught
Quivers in your green eyes as if in wrack hung pools. But
    floating

We drift apart, or groan, like moored unfendered boats,
Starting our broken sides, where the brackish influx pours:
We fly at dawns or breaks at one another's throats
And nothing natural nor art can ease this bitterness of ours.

The Return

Four days we did not speak, tried to pretend
This time we'd bring this marriage to an end,
Consulting train timetables, considering where
We could divide our chattels, share by share,
Correcting our 'ours', biting our lips on 'we',
Calling this house 'mine', expounding bitterly
Who should leave whom, with whom the children should
Stay, until it seemed as if this time had come for good,
The break had come. Neither could humble pride,
Mollify hate, come timidly confessing wrong.
The days dragged slowly harrowing along,
The nights all tautness in our limbs and ears,
Broken with fugitive retreats, uneasy fears.
Meanwhile you blossomed womanly, a brightening crown
Brushed in your hair, dress shoulder would slip down,
Painted your toes, you moved your hips in poise
Making our home shine, filling the place with noise,
Piano-preludes, stories for the children, dust
Flying woebegone, laundry line-tossed,
Then again in basketfuls come sweet and dry
While swirl the willow skirts and the uncertain summer sky
Throws lights across your polished floors and our
Home patterns. Now I cease to glower

My fit reverts to its original anxiety, and then
Turns to destructive: I shout at you again
And as this leaves my lips I hear the cold echo
Of a man left alone between these walls, and know
How much I love you, suddenly, like a pulled tendon, taut
Runs the touched nerve. I can see that you are hurt,
And yet I will not humble me: as I pass by
Silent, withdrawn, my belly heaves, heart gives a sigh
My body wrestles like a captive in a net,
Heart, mind, compassion fight me strenuously, yet:
I dare not let them free. Until you lift the phone,
And I must plead for amnesty. Bruised, in a stun
Our day goes by, then the return of trust
Restores romantic softnesses, that rise away to lust.

I watched the water spring this morning wondering
At its continual fullness as each ripple ring
Spread from the source, at the continual wave
That wells restoring by such waterlights. The peace you gave
Flows thus back round our home: in this fresh lake
Our children dance, the blue kingfisher streaks, the waterflowers
    awake.

OUT OF THIS WORLD. II

A Beach in Galloway

No, there is nothing by which we may organise
Dreadful Port Counan Beach into a scheme.
It is. Glad to be viable a while with eyes
We thank the unbelievable wild accident, and climb
Back along furry rocks and slimy ledges where
The tide cannot outflank us, and there
Intend to light a driftwood fire and fry.
But each stick that we gather moans aloud,
Until at the small chimney where we try
White water-logging ghosts predate us in a crowd.
And so, our reasons never spoken, we return
To climb the cliff-path hurriedly by van,
Leaving a solitary oyster-catcher with his tabs of red
Crying the crown of ghosts, watched by a lonely seal, among the
    dead.

There an old single bull seal ducks and bobs
Among the winches and sea-polished plates
And a round sea-beached boiler. That summer day
Down a zig on the map we drove on stones,
Then walked under the rocks' tilt-ends, where violence
Far beyond the capacity of mind to grasp
Blew pumice, squeezed up marble veins, squashed slate,
Stacked, folded, ruptured, cut, burst, then,
Raised, weathered, sea-rubbed, broke and sanded—there
Was what they call a port—a drift
Between dead rock and water; water, rock. A beach
Footless as we now foot it. Clean,
Except for baulks and roots, mast-lengths, splint stuff,
Piled wave-culled sea-weed, chalk whorl-cabins. Then,
As we look closer, rivets, tins and bones,
Sheeps' vertebrae, men's ribs, and printed messages,
On tin and wood and canvas relics, messageless
Gunwhales unrecognisable, small hooks, shoes, shreds,

29

Among the cluttered stones, between the pools, above
Where the cliffs crack or round, and sea
Laps into splits and throats or bowls, or edges face.

More than a small crab stripped of its housing shell
By accident, as we stirred pebbles in a pool,
Counts none of us, says Counan. The crab splays and dies,
The children watch the live ones as they try to hide,
Mimicking stones and shadows: so we forget.
'I know,' says she who smashed the green crablet.
'Look! There's a 'nemone with its feelers out!'
Green haired ship's irons are the only grave
Of those whom they in breaking carried under the wave,
Leaving a rib and shoe only that don't remember
What hope strained to the end one dark night in December.

Words cannot give account of all
The coloured convolutions of that rock,
Nor what I learnt from them, the little while
We marked the vacant beach with our stray vagrant walk.
Here continents like sugar-candy boils
Felt the crust cooling in a moon-torn lock
Then burst with planet-shifting moils
Throwing out noiseless comet-dusts of rock.
What saved this entity of earth when seas
Emptied or filled, when Galloway
Was split from Ireland, or when these
Mountains to Counan sands were worn away?

Here a small white-haired boy, my son,
Squints at a seal. My second daughter cries
Because the mile-long waste of rock all stinks,
Sand-fly covered, their hopping herds on wrack,
Half-decayed sea-weed, with sharp pungent breaths
Of dead crabs' claws, skate eggs, and jelly-fish.
My elder daughter, climbing on the rocks
Tremblingly stalks under cracked hanging stones
To gog at pale green ferns within a cave. And she,

30

My love, her hair all sea-salt, slim,
Her small back beautiful, goes down to swim
Dwarfed by the ugly plates where ship torn cries
Were uttered once unheard, their last of civilise.

Cold in a cave once sat Saint Ninian there
Gazing at Counan Beach as I do now
Some twenty thousand months ago, in some dark year—
Barbarians over Europe, Gallia to Greece,
Britain still Saxon, a few scattered devotees
Westwards still keeping vows and discipline.
Only a fraction of an inch has that rock worn
Since his faith came to captivate
With hope against the crushing weight
Of all such rocky evidence that man counts less
Than anything worth saving by a God in mortal dress.
There he brought first the story, back the hope
From storm-swept Ireland, of an afterlife, a God
Who planned all things, even wild Counan beach. Grope
We as then where Ninian spent retreat, and trod
That fawn mashed silica where winch and bones,
Seals, cans and broken strata crumble all
Tossed round in Time with us, the holidaying ones
Who see the four-ring crosses cut in his cave wall.

Hopeless Oh saint we run
From veins of coloured stone
To red anemone
Or the white seaman's bone.

Four circles on a stone
Delineate your cross
Saving a saint from loss:
Only a stone or bone

Pick we from Whithorn's case,
Or see in the rifled tombs
In the saint's place,
Or here where the wind combs,

31

Sea combs, beachcombings; time
Smooths warted rocks, erodes
Walls you could contemplate as God's,
Stones which contempt us, are sublime

Accidents that we cannot now explain,
Except as 'happening' from igneous to rain,
Between the pretend beginning of the world, and here,
Where we succeed you on this beach, this year.

(St. Ninian, a native of Galloway, was the first to bring Christianity to
the mainland of Britain from Ireland. He established a chapel at Whithorn, Wigtownshire, in A.D. 397, and had a chapel at Isle of Whithorn,
and a cave on the shore. At Whithorn Priory is a fine collection of
carved stones, and excavations at Priory have brought to light chalices
and rings from later periods, now in Edinburgh Museum.)

Printed in Great Britain by Richard Clay and Company Ltd.,
Bungay, Suffolk